HOW TO **PLAN YOUR DOCTORATE JOURNEY** SMARTLY

HOW TO **PLAN YOUR DOCTORATE JOURNEY** SMARTLY

A COMPLETE GUIDE FOR WORKING PROFESSIONALS TO GET STARTED WITH A PhD PROGRAM

Dr Raman K. Attri

Copyrights © 2021 Raman K Attri and Speed To Proficiency Research: S2Pro©

All rights reserved. No part of this publication may be reproduced, distributed, or transmitted in any form or by any means, including photocopying, recording, or other electronic or mechanical methods, without the prior written permission of the author and publisher, except in the case of brief quotations embodied in critical reviews and certain other noncommercial uses permitted by copyright law.

ISBN: 978-981-18-4293-1 (e-book)
ISBN: 978-981-18-4291-7 (paperback)
ISBN: 978-981-18-4292-4 (hardcover)

Published in Singapore
Printed in the United States of America / Australia / UK

https://www.speedtoproficiency.com
info@speedtoproficiency.com

National Library Board, Singapore Cataloguing in Publication Data

Name(s): Attri, Raman K., 1973-
Title: How to plan your doctorate journey smartly : a complete guide for working professionals to get started with a PhD program / Dr Raman K. Attri.
Description: Singapore : Speed To Proficiency Research, [2022]
Identifier(s): ISBN 978-981-18-4291-7 (Paperback) | 978-981-18-4292-4 (Hardback) | 978-981-18-4293-1 (Epub)
Subject(s): LCSH: Doctor of philosophy degree. | Universities and colleges-- Graduate work.
Classification: DDC 378.24--dc23

Edited by: Anupama Natarajan

Distilled wisdom for working professionals from a corporate learning executive who lived the doctoral cycle twice

To Dr Wing S. Wu for guiding me through my doctoral journey

AUTHOR

Dr Raman K. Attri is a multifaceted personality as a scientist, author, speaker, L&D leader, and artist. Recognized as a Brainz Global 500 leader among stellar personalities like Oprah Winfrey, Gary Vee, Jim Kwik, and Jim Shetty, he is the world's leading authority on the "science of speed" in professional learning and performance. A performance scientist with over two decades of research, he has created a time-tested, proven system that can help leaders and organizations to positively speed up the path to mastery and leadership in any domain by two folds.

Permanently disabled since childhood, he is often called a powerhouse of positivity and inspiration. He transformed his inability to walk into unique expertise to teach people how to walk faster in their professional world.

Among his most recent projects is the 'GetThereFaster' portal, a one-stop resource for anyone to learn the secrets of learning better and faster.

A professional speaker, he shares research-based insights at leading international conferences with top business executives to master speed in business, shorten workforce time to proficiency, and accelerate employee development.

A global training thought leader at a Fortune 500 technology corporation, he manages one of the world's top 10 Hall of the Fame training organization.

A prolific author of 22 multigenre books, he writes books and articles on various topics ranging from business & leadership, performance & expertise, and training & development to HR & workforce development.

Passionate about continuous learning, he has earned two doctorates in learning, over 100 international educational credentials, several degrees and diplomas, and some of the highest certifications. He is an authentic accelerated learning business coach who walks the talk.

Featured in over 125 articles, interviews, and shows, he is a highly sought-after expert whose remarkable achievements continue to inspire everyone he touches to strive for true excellence in their personal and professional lives.

LinkedIn: https://linkedin.com/in/DrRamanKAttri

Facebook: https://facebook.com/DrRamanKAttri

Website: http://ramankattri.com

Contact: contact@ramankattri.com

PREFACE

Taking up a doctorate sets you apart from the rest. It establishes you as an authority or specialist in a specific field of human endeavors. It makes you come across as a knowledgeable and go-to person. Having a prestigious doctorate on your profile makes you more available in the market and presents you as a critical differentiator.

If you are at a turning-point stage in your corporate management career, where you are actively thinking of attaining the highest level of educational degree to create that extra edge in your career, then this book is for you.

While most universities have comprehensive documentation, support, and infrastructure to make your journey smooth, taking the first step becomes the biggest challenge for most working professionals and managers.

Things do not always turn out what one may expect in the beginning. Therefore, it is imperative that you make the right decisions to begin with, and then plan your journey smartly.

In this book, Dr. Raman K Attri shares his personal experience and research on making the right decisions. Having completed two doctorates in a brief period, Dr. Raman will guide you through how to plan for this daunting path effortlessly. This book answers the mysteries and behind-the-scenes truth of attaining a doctorate with reasonably less-taxing efforts. Through several reflective questions embedded in the book, the readers will be able to assess if taking up a doctorate path is the right decision for them.

This book is specially designed for working professionals, corporate managers, executives, and management leaders. In this book, you will be able to learn:

1) identify the skills, competencies, and expertise required to undertake successful doctorate research,
2) Identify how you can leverage your current and previous practice-based experience and translate that into doctorate research.

While this book is complete in itself, I encourage readers to check out my learning portal https://get-there-faster.com to learn about more resources and register for online courses to get into the depth of the content.

All the best for your journey.

Let's get there faster, together!

Dr Raman K Attri

June 2022

CONTENTS

CHAPTER 1
INTRODUCTION

1.1	ONE-WAY JOURNEY	3
1.2	KEY TAKEAWAYS	3
1.3	LEARNING OBJECTIVES	4
1.4	JOURNEY	4
1.5	FINAL THOUGHTS	5

CHAPTER 2
UNDERSTANDING YOUR MOTIVES AND DRIVERS

2.1	UNDERSTANDING THE WORTH	9
2.2	SMART CHOICES	11
2.3	SET THE IMPRESSION	12
2.4	START WITH WHY	14
2.5	KNOW THE VALUE	17
2.5.1	VALUE TO YOU	19
2.5.2	VALUE TO ORGANIZATIONS	22
2.6	DEFINE THE VALUE	25
2.6.1	VALUE FOR YOUR PRACTICE OR CAREER	25
2.6.2	LONG-TERM VALUE (>14 YEARS)	25
2.6.3	EVERGREEN	26
2.6.4	MAIN PRODUCT	28
2.6.5	BY-PRODUCTS	29

| 2.7 | MAKING SMART CHOICES | 31 |

CHAPTER 3
NAVIGATING THE ANATOMY OF A DOCTORATE JOURNEY

3.1	CHOOSING THE STRUCTURE		35
	3.1.1	BY FOCUS	35
	3.1.2	BY TENURE	35
	3.1.3	BY STRUCTURE	35
	3.1.4	BY ASSESSMENT	36
	3.1.5	BY MODE	38
	3.1.6	PhD vs PROFESSIONAL DOCTORATE	38
	3.1.7	CONSIDER ALL FACTORS	41
3.2	ESTIMATE THE TIME		42
	3.2.1	THESIS WORK	43
	3.2.2	ASSESSMENT WORK	44
	3.2.3	PREPARING FOR A BOOK	45
3.3	ASSESS THE LEVEL OF EFFORTS		46
	3.3.1	LEARNING NEW SKILLS	50
	3.3.2	WORK-LIFE BALANCE	50
	3.3.3	READING ARTICLES ENDLESSLY	51
3.4	FIGURE OUT THE SKILLS		52
	3.4.1	PROFESSIONAL SKILLS	54
	3.4.2	PERSONAL SKILLS	57
3.5	STAY OPEN TO FEEDBACK		60

CHAPTER 4
ASSESSING YOUR BEST BETS AND LEVERAGES

4.1	KNOW YOUR PERSONALITY	63
4.2	LEVERAGE YOUR BEST BETS	67
4.2.1	GOAL-ORIENTED MANAGEMENT	67
4.2.2	PRAGMATIC APPROACHES	67
4.2.3	SYSTEMS THINKING	68
4.3	FIND THE KEY LEVERAGES	70
4.3.1	TECHNOLOGICAL LEVERAGES	70
4.3.2	ECOSYSTEM LEVERAGES	72
4.3.3	PERSONAL LEVERAGES	74
4.4	PERSONALITY & ECOSYSTEM	77

CHAPTER 5
HOW TO START THE JOURNEY WITH THE END IN MIND

5.1	CHOOSE THE RIGHT MODE	81
5.1.1	TYPE	81
5.1.2	STRUCTURE	81
5.1.3	TENURE	82
5.1.4	UNIVERSITY	82
5.1.5	STANDING	82
5.1.6	MODE	83
5.1.7	THESIS SUPERVISOR	83

5.1.8	LIBRARY RESOURCES	84
5.1.9	ASSESSMENT	85
5.2	SELECT A CREDIBLE AREA OF RESEARCH	86
5.2.1	SIGNIFICANT CAREER STREAMS	88
5.2.2	TOP-NOTCH SKILLS OR SPECIALIZATION	88
5.2.3	AUTHORITY, EXPERTISE, OR CREDENTIALS	88
5.2.4	INTELLECTUAL PROPERTY CREATED	88
5.2.5	AUTHORSHIPS OR PUBLICATIONS	89
5.2.6	PASSIONS OR MOTIVATIONS	89
5.2.7	FUTURE PROSPECTS	90
5.3	SELECTING A REWARDING TOPIC	93
5.3.1	TOPIC AUTHORITY: WHY YOU?	95
5.3.2	RESEARCH AUTHORITY: WHY THIS WAY?	95
5.3.3	MOTIVATIONS AND DRIVERS: WHY DO IT?	95
5.3.4	ECOSYSTEM: WHY ONLY THIS?	96
5.3.5	EFFORTS: WHY NOT THIS?	97
5.4	MAKE SMART CHOICES	103

CHAPTER 6
WHAT IS NEXT?

6.1	RESEARCH FRAMEWORK	107
6.2	ONLINE COURSE	109

CHAPTER 1

INTRODUCTION

INTRODUCTION

Earning a doctorate sets you apart from the rest. It establishes you as an authority or specialist in a specific field. It makes you come across as a knowledgeable and go-to person. Having a prestigious doctorate in your profile makes you more available in the market and presents you as a critical differentiator. If you are at a turning-point stage in your corporate management career, where you are actively thinking of attaining the highest level of educational degree to create that extra edge in your career, then this book is for you.

A PhD or doctorate is a big decision in life, and it doesn't come easy. We keep waiting for that signal that assures us that this is the right time to go on such a long journey. However, part of this game is your maturity and confidence, where you feel, 'Yeah, I'm ready; I need to embark on this journey.' Also, you need to wait for your experience to become ripe enough so that you can ride upon it and use it. Or, maybe, sometimes, we think of doing a doctorate because we feel that it is the time of that competition in the market, and that we need to differentiate ourselves. "Cost" is an important factor in the doctoral journey because some doctoral programs easily cost $100k; even more in some institutions. So, you need to have a big pocket and immense courage.

I am a business and learning researcher. I hold two doctorates. I have gone through that painful cycle not once but twice. During my journey, I have accumulated immense experience and insight, which I am sharing in this book. I intend to guide you through how to plan for this daunting path. I have served as a scientist, so I have a fair understanding of the research cycle. In this book, I present collective wisdom from my personal experience and research on making the right decisions. The book reveals some not-so-obvious facts and the behind-the-scene truths of attaining a doctorate, with reasonably less-taxing efforts. Based on the several reflective sessions embedded in this book, you will, for yourself, be able to assess whether taking up the path to a doctorate is the right thing for you.

The crux of the book is to enable you to make smart choices while taking up a doctoral program. The book will force you to reflect upon—Are you ready to take up this journey or not?

1.1   ONE-WAY JOURNEY

The path to a doctorate is a one-way street. Once you start, there should be no turning back. You've got only two choices: either quit or finish. Because if you leave it midway, it will not give you any value, and you're going to possibly feel bad about your decision because it is lots and lots of effort. You may take some diversions during your PhD, like changing a topic, changing your supervisor, or probably changing the location. But there is no stopping or turning back after stepping into this journey.

1.2   KEY TAKEAWAYS

Identify the skills, competencies, and expertise required to undertake successful doctoral research.

1) Identify how you can leverage your current and previous practice-based experience

INTRODUCTION

2) Translate that into a doctoral research study.

1.3 LEARNING OBJECTIVES

- Understand and identify your drives and career goals
- Understand the complete picture of a typical doctoral journey
- Assess how a doctorate is a right choice for your career
- Identify the potential challenges and pitfalls of pursuing the doctorate
- Identify and analyze the skills required to complete the doctorate
- Self-assess your readiness to undertake the doctoral journey
- Develop a decision matrix to help you prioritize your goals, decisions, and timing
- Choose the pathway requiring minimal effort as a working professional
- Finish a part-time doctorate successfully alongside your day job
- Prepare a plan for your doctoral journey

1.4 JOURNEY

I have set up this book as a journey. There are basically four segments, as shown in Figure 1-1.

PLAN YOUR DOCTORATE JOURNEY SMARTLY

In the first segment, we will talk about why we wish to take up this journey.

In the second segment, we will talk about how long the overall journey will take, how difficult it is, the other challenges you will face, and the other aspects that you ideally need to know before you embark on that journey.

In the third segment, we will discuss the skills/virtues to be assessed, such as whether you have what it takes to complete the doctoral journey. That is because there are several skills that you're going to need to embark on this journey.

And in the fourth and the last segment, we'll discuss "if all goes well, how do you start your journey?"

1.5 FINAL THOUGHTS

In the end, I would like to express my respect for your longing to get more knowledge and develop your intellectual skills by taking up a daunting journey in pursuit of a doctorate. That's probably one of the main reasons you're reading this book. Good luck and flourish while using the nuggets and tips spread in this book.

INTRODUCTION

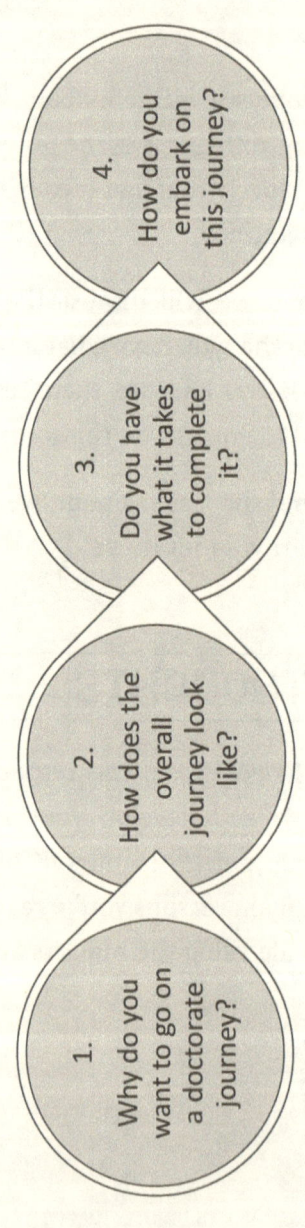

Figure 1-1: Doctorate journey described through four segments

CHAPTER 2

UNDERSTANDING YOUR MOTIVES AND DRIVERS

YOUR MOTIVES AND DRIVERS

In this introductory section, you will be put into a reflection mode to explore or investigate your drivers and motives to take up a doctoral journey. The module starts by bringing out your thoughts on someone who has already gained such a credential. You will learn about the various forces acting as your drivers to go for such a challenging program. The lesson will allow you to identify values or benefits the credential and research can bring to you, your family, and your profession.

PLAN YOUR DOCTORATE JOURNEY SMARTLY

2.1 UNDERSTANDING THE WORTH

Analyzing if the journey is worth the effort

There are several opinions out there in the market on whether a doctorate is still relevant.

To answer that, we use the Cornell University data corresponding to 2020. While the data pertain chiefly to Australia, the figures can be applied to other countries as well since the global situation is pretty similar. It may be observed that there has been a steady rise in the number of PhDs in the last 70 years.

As shown in Figure 2-1, the line of interest is line number 1, which shows the cumulative number of PhDs in Australia. I can say that the global situation is quite similar. In a large country like Australia itself, there are only 200,000 doctoral degree holders against its total population. In reality, the number of doctorates in any country is a tiny fraction of its workforce, which also means that there are only going to be a handful of doctoral degree holders in your proximity. It's not everyone's cup of tea, right? That's why there is a fascination with this program.

YOUR MOTIVES AND DRIVERS

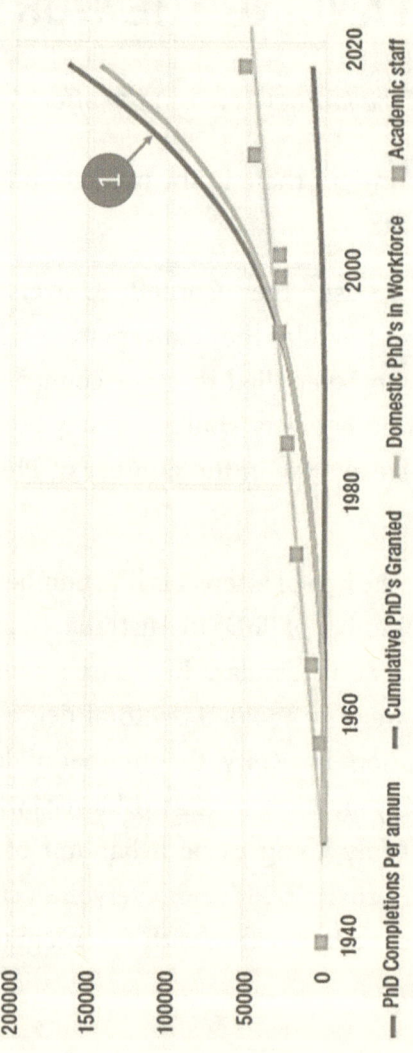

Figure 2.1: Trends in PhD completions and academic workforce

[source: https://gradschool.cornell.edu/about/program-metrics-assessments-and-outcomes/doctoral-career-outcomes/]

2.2 SMART CHOICES

A "doctorate" or "doctoral degree" is the highest academic degree in any field/subject area. So, it's pretty normal for anybody to think that it will provide them the competitive differentiation. At the same time, you might also believe that a doctorate could be your X-factor. However, the hard truth is that it is not always going to be an X-factor. Not every degree will add a competitive edge to your profession, job, or business. To get that level of differentiation, you are going to need to make some smart choices, combined with the opportunities and the ecosystem surrounding you. When you make those smart choices, your decision to do a doctorate can become a competitive edge for you.

2.3 SET THE IMPRESSION

Appreciating how the doctorate credential is viewed by others

Let's begin with the following questions: Why do you want to do a doctorate in the first place? What is in this credential that is basically attracting you? Before I did my doctorate, I used to view this degree as the epitome of knowledge. I had the impression that "doctorate" folks hold the highest status in corporate, professional, and scientific domains. However, that is not really true. Having a doctorate is not a sure-shot way to go up.

Reflect on these for a moment and capture your notes in Reflection 2.1.

- How do you view the "doctorate" credential?
- What comes to your mind when you hear someone has earned a doctorate?
- How do your peers' view someone with such a credential?

Some believe that "a person holding such a degree is an expert in his topic of interest." In fact, people will view you as an expert in that particular topic because a "doctorate" is the topmost academic qualification. You would be considered to have a deep understanding of that topic (in some cases, the domain). You would have studied for years and years on one specific topic or issue. You would be considered an authority in that particular topic you have researched.

PLAN YOUR DOCTORATE JOURNEY SMARTLY

Reflection 2.1

How do you view doctorate credentials? What comes to your mind when you hear someone has a doctorate? How do you think others like your peers' view someone with such a credential?

_____
_____
_____
_____
_____
_____
_____
_____
_____
_____
_____
_____
_____
_____
_____
_____
_____
_____
_____

2.4 START WITH WHY

*Finding out your drivers and the "why"
behind your goals*

Sometimes, I reflect and think about why I did it. Not once, but twice! As I think back, I realize that there must have been a strong motivational force or push-pull factor behind it. As I go back to my childhood memories, I see myself as someone who would chase "how-to" methods to do anything. When I was a child, I used to read books, which started with "how-to." That was always my first choice. I wanted to know how things are done in personal and professional settings and how some are better than others.

The curiosity to know about things became my personal "why." In my first doctorate, I focused on "how to" teach complex problem-solving to employees to help them navigate the complex business world they are in. In my second doctorate, I was highly interested in understanding "how to" make employees or professionals as experts in their jobs and make them work in a shorter time.

So, there are always some "why" drivers or motives that push you, pull you, or appeal to you somehow. There are different aspects of why somebody would want to go for a doctorate. Maybe we are attracted to that topic, or we have seen others exercising more authority because of the doctorate title, or we carry an impression that they are the topmost experts. Thus, there can be several such drivers for you.

PLAN YOUR DOCTORATE JOURNEY SMARTLY

Look deep inside yourself and take a moment to reflect upon these questions, and capture your notes in Reflection 2.2:

- Why do you think about it?
- What are your personal drives?
- What is your "why"?
- Why do you want to go on such an arduous journey?

YOUR MOTIVES AND DRIVERS

Reflection 2.2

Why do you think about it? What are your personal drives? What is your "why"? Why do you want to go on such an arduous journey?

2.5 KNOW THE VALUE

Assessing the value from two different viewpoints

The key aspect to understand is the value it offers. Reflect on these questions and capture your notes in Reflection 2.3.

- What advantages do you expect from earning a doctorate?
- What value are you hoping to get for yourself by obtaining a doctorate?

While reflecting on these, think of its value to your own self, your family, your profession, your community, your employer, or your business.

There are two different lenses or viewpoints which you can use to assess the value. One from your own angle, and the other, from an organization's angle.

YOUR MOTIVES AND DRIVERS

Reflection 2.3

What advantages do you expect from earning a doctorate? What value are you hoping to get for yourself by obtaining a doctorate? Think of value to yourself, your family, profession, community, employer, or your business.

_____
_____
_____
_____
_____
_____
_____
_____
_____
_____
_____
_____
_____
_____
_____
_____
_____
_____
_____

PLAN YOUR DOCTORATE JOURNEY SMARTLY

2.5.1 VALUE TO YOU

*Figuring out two views of finding value—
Current vs. Future*

I realize that a doctorate may have two value propositions depending on how one views it, as shown in **Figure 2.2**.

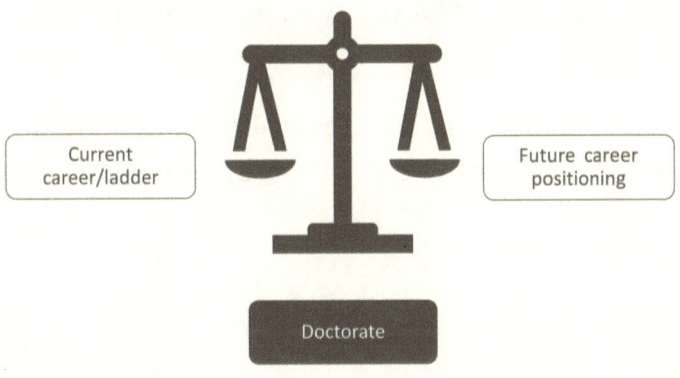

Figure 2.2: Assessing the value of the doctoral program from one's own viewpoint.

One is, when you do this to line it up with your current specialization or career and want to speed up what you are doing right now. If that is how you want, the choices you make later in the journey will have a lot of bearing.

The second is that you have some dream idea that is probably based on your past or current experience, or it could be a breakthrough realization you think is for you to explore. It could

YOUR MOTIVES AND DRIVERS

be an intuition that something will be of more value in the future. Then you choose the idea to become that expert. If this describes you, then your choices are going to be a lot different.

However, the journey to earning a doctorate is a one-way street. That means you have to be absolutely sure about your current or future positioning. In my case, I tried to do the one which was already a large part of my current career; so, I possibly had no conflict between my present and future aspirations. But that may not be the case with everyone.

Reflect on this for a while and capture your notes in Reflection 2.4.

- The value you hope to receive—is it geared toward your current career progression or future positioning?

PLAN YOUR DOCTORATE JOURNEY SMARTLY

Reflection 2.4

Think about whether the value you hope to receive—is geared toward your current career progression or future positioning?

YOUR MOTIVES AND DRIVERS

2.5.2 VALUE TO ORGANIZATIONS

Understanding the three types of outcomes valued in organizations

Although it is important to consider the value that you may obtain after earning a doctorate, in your current position or in the future, the degree needs to generate outcomes that an organization values. The organization can be your employer, client, or even your own business.

In my experience, three kinds of ideas are valued the most in organizations, as summarized in Figure 2.3.

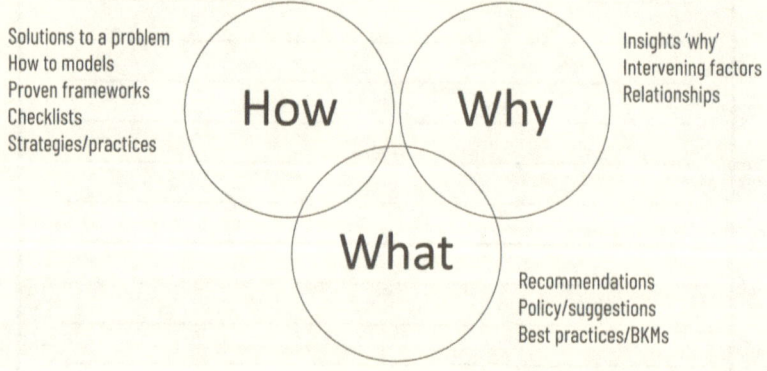

Figure 2.3: Value of a doctoral program for organizations.

1) How

The first one is focused on HOW—How to solve a critical problem, for instance, manager's efficiency. Such practice-oriented research focuses on finding how-to models, proven

PLAN YOUR DOCTORATE JOURNEY SMARTLY

frameworks, checklists, or strategies to solve problems. For instance, in my second PhD, I have delivered 24 strategies and 6 proven business practices used by over 50 organizations to shorten time to proficiency. These are high-value outcomes that can make you "sought after" instantly within your own organization.

2) Why

The second one is focused on WHY—which includes insightful revelations, factors, and relationships; why do things happen the way they do? For example, in my research, I also found why training and learning actually hampered the acceleration of proficiency. Again, these are high-value outcomes that can correct the course of action in an organization.

3) What

The third is about WHAT—which is focused on recommendations, best practices in terms of what works, and sometimes policy instruments.

In my experience, if corporate professionals chase some abstract ideas, and build theories that may not immediately apply in a business or organizational settings, you are going to have challenges finding the right people to support, take part, and review.

Reflect on this for a moment and capture your notes in Reflection 2.5.

- What is your assessment of the intended program by assessing for yourself and for your organization?

YOUR MOTIVES AND DRIVERS

Reflection 2.5

What is your assessment of the intended program by assessing for yourself and for your organization?

PLAN YOUR DOCTORATE JOURNEY SMARTLY

2.6 DEFINE THE VALUE

*Using the 5-point method to assess the value
you hope to produce*

We talked about the value a doctorate may have for your employer, but, the important point is how earning the degree could contribute to speeding up your career. At the end of the day, the doctorate needs to produce value for you, right?

I recommend using 5-point criteria to assess the value you could hope to create out of your doctoral program. The criteria are shown in Figure 2.4. It is not just about having a title, but you need to be able to live off this value for the rest of your professional career.

2.6.1   VALUE FOR YOUR PRACTICE OR CAREER

In the last segment, you used two viewpoints, one comprising current vs. future value and another one comprising "How," "Why," and "What" components of strategies are valuable to the business or organization. These are the factors that give you an understanding of the value your doctoral degree is potentially going to create, which can help you in your practice or career.

2.6.2   LONG-TERM VALUE (>14 YEARS)

There are a few things you need to consider to understand the long-term value of your program. Imagine you spend 7 to 8 years

YOUR MOTIVES AND DRIVERS

of your life earning this degree. However, if the outcome, model, theory, and knowledge you create in this process do not live for at least 7 more years, it may not be the right investment. If you are to spend 7 years trying to discover something, its value better persists for several more years. That is why, I emphasize that there must be a long-term value of minimum of 14 to 15 years from the day you start the program.

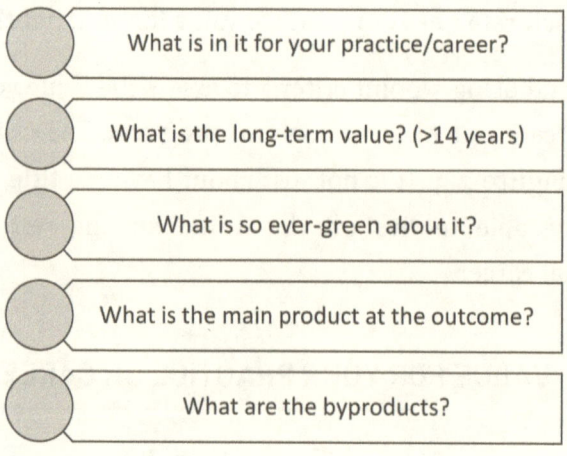

Figure 2.4: Five-point criteria to define the value of your doctoral program.

2.6.3 EVERGREEN

When we start such a program, we are too focused on contemporary, current issues. Even on social media, most of the things that we discuss are related to the present or are important in the present. The shelf life of those issues is short. Most of us

PLAN YOUR DOCTORATE JOURNEY SMARTLY

work in companies where, most of the time, we are busy solving immediate problems. Such problems are the ones that appeal to us so much that we take them to our PhD or doctoral research because we don't think about their applicability 7 or 8 years later.

While your supervisors and university may be focused on immediate, known, or emerging problems as great candidates for doctoral research, you need to assess the topic or idea, or the applicability of earning your doctorate in one specific specialization based on its future value.

You are going to take not less than 7 years to explore the idea you pick today. You need to think whether 'irrespective of the idea you explore in this 7-year period, is it going to be relevant after 7 years?' If not, all the hard work you are going to do may not give you the value you had in mind when you started.

For example, you may choose a topic such as "how artificial intelligence (AI) can change the way management works?" or something along those lines. That's great! Organizations are not waiting for your PhD to be completed to innovate. They consistently invest their resources in creating new strategies. So, the odds are that, by the time you work on an idea and come out with something wonderful 7 or 8 years later, it may be already prevalent in the market to the extent that you would struggle to position your leadership in that area. Or, perhaps, by the time you bring your unique findings or recommendations through your thesis into the market, multinational corporations like IBM or Microsoft may even have come up with supercomputing cloud-based solutions that can enable managerial decision-making in seconds.

YOUR MOTIVES AND DRIVERS

But you may probably be better off by focusing on topics like "how AI can help large organizations or CEOs make fullproof decisions related to mergers and acquisitions (M&A)? However, that is a niche topic, a very specific and perhaps a more evergreen topic, as M&A is never going to go out of fashion or demand. They are going to be applicable even years later.

Thus, the real value of earning a PhD comes when you think beyond immediate needs. When you think about a problem you're going to solve, not just something that is surrounding you today but something that you foresee even after a few years or even a decade. The long-term value of your PhD is, therefore, very, very important.

My definition of "evergreenness" is that the idea you're going to work on must persist for at least 14 years, which includes the 7 years that you are going to explore it. You then probably take another 7 years to get the commercial or business value out of it. So, keep a total of 14 years' time horizon in mind.

Therefore, I would highly encourage you to figure out what you are going to produce that will be evergreen.

The world is changing fast. By the time you complete the doctoral program, will your research outcome still be applicable to the changed world at that time?

2.6.4   MAIN PRODUCT

You need to think of the product that you produce at the outcome when you finish the degree. Is it a model, theory, or knowledge?

PLAN YOUR DOCTORATE JOURNEY SMARTLY

2.6.5 BY-PRODUCTS

What by-products are you hoping to produce from your doctorate? Sometimes, by-products are much more valuable than the main product itself. The main product may be 300 pages on an idea. But then, by-products can be your books and/or consulting practices; can help you license out your finding(s) to somebody; or can be your public speaking career. Do think about by-products.

Reflect on this for a moment and capture your notes in Reflection 2.6.

- Are you thinking about an evergreen idea?
- Are you considering long-term beyond 14 years also?
- Are you trying to solve a problem, or do you want to explore the problem which has a long-term appeal to organizations and the community?

YOUR MOTIVES AND DRIVERS

Reflection 2.6

Are you thinking about an evergreen idea? Are you considering long-term beyond 14 years also? Are you trying to solve a problem, or do you want to explore the problem which has long-term appeal to organizations and in the community?

2.7 MAKING SMART CHOICES

In the end, I would like to share a learning insight. Going for a doctorate and then completing it is a matter of smart choices that need to be grounded in your "why" motives in terms of your reason to do it, the value you hope to receive, and the value you hope to add.

CHAPTER 3

NAVIGATING THE ANATOMY OF A DOCTORATE JOURNEY

THE ANATOMY OF A DOCTORATE JOURNEY

In this chapter, you will deep dive into understanding the various ways universities set up doctoral programs and what they mean to you in terms of effort, investment, and time. This chapter will enable you to be realistic about the time and effort you will need to spend to complete a doctoral program. Lastly, you will assess a range of skills that are considered important to complete the doctoral program with flying colors. This chapter will reveal to you certain implicit parameters that you may not have thought about before.

PLAN YOUR DOCTORATE JOURNEY SMARTLY

3.1 CHOOSING THE STRUCTURE

Choosing the path or structure of the program wisely

There are multiple paths to earning a doctorate, as summarized in Figure 3-1.

3.1.1   BY FOCUS

The first one is by focus—do you want to do an academic doctorate like a PhD (Doctor of Philosophy) or a professional doctorate? I will explain the differences later in this module.

3.1.2   BY TENURE

Now, there are again two types based on tenure. Full-time is certainly not a choice for working professionals. You will go part-time, which usually runs for twice the length of the full-time. You're going to need to look for a part-time one.

3.1.3   BY STRUCTURE

There are paths based on how the program is structured. The two most common ones are:

(1) The first is purely only courses of deeper nature, and, in some cases, has a project as a subject for 6 months or so. It is pretty

much a reading/exam/assessment-intensive structure. However, since this path will give you only a degree and you may not come out wiser than before, it may not be the right choice if you hope to build a commercial value model or research.

(2) The second is the usual structure comprising an intense set of courses such as qualitative methods, quantitative methods, statistics, and project proposal that help you build your research foundation. It also includes a deeper level of the thesis that runs for several years and has research value. Depending upon your past qualifications, you may get waivers for coursework.

Some universities offer research-only tracks for scientists and scholars who are not new to the research.

3.1.4   BY ASSESSMENT

Different doctoral programs follow different ways of carrying out assessments.

A more usual or traditional PhD is where you need to write your thesis. However, the success of this path depends on how well you defend and argue verbally in front of a doctoral committee.

Another type of PhD is where the quality of the written thesis and content, rationale, methods, data, etc. are reviewed by professors who are authorities in the corresponding subject area; an in-person interview is, however, not conducted. However, this mode is writing-intensive. But it can work great for guys who have reasonable writing skills.

PLAN YOUR DOCTORATE JOURNEY SMARTLY

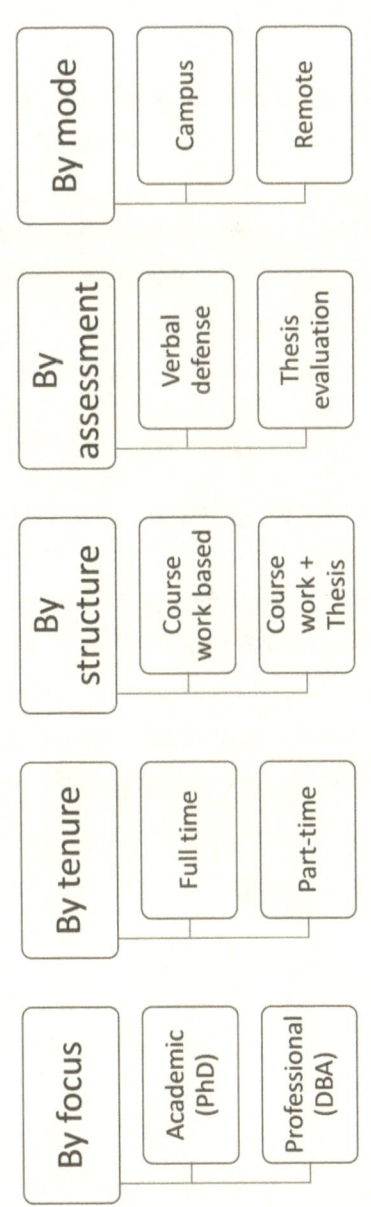

Figure 3-1: Parameters defining program structure

3.1.5 BY MODE

Then, of course, you may have the possibility to go on the campus in the country where the university is located or you may be able to do it via their in-country campuses. For example, Australia, USA, Canada, and UK universities have established their remote campuses in several countries. Education has no boundary these days. I did my PhD from one of the universities in Australia, but the university has a well-established infrastructure in Singapore too.

3.1.6 PhD vs PROFESSIONAL DOCTORATE

These days, universities are offering two kinds of programs: (1) PhD, which is "Doctor of Philosophy" and (2) professional doctorate. The professional doctorate is a relatively new degree but should nowadays be completely respected. It has already started getting a wider reach in corporate circles.

PLAN YOUR DOCTORATE JOURNEY SMARTLY

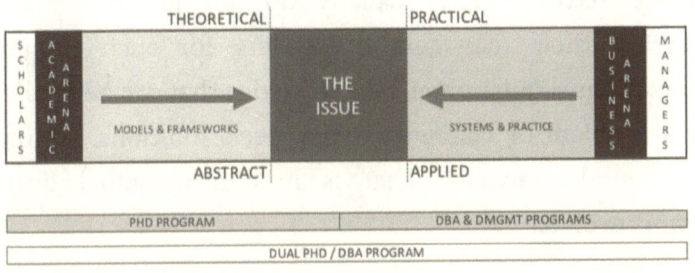

Figure 3-2: PhD versus DBA programs.

The problem with the academic PhD program is that apart from being highly intense and difficult, it also tends to be theoretical and abstract if the degree is pursued in subject areas such as social sciences, management, and business. Such a degree focuses on finding out theories, models, or frameworks, which could explain certain phenomena. However, in the case of academic PhD programs, the emphasis is more on creating hard-core researchers and not informed practitioners. Also, in the first place, you've got to demonstrate to be a researcher of great quality to seek admission into the program. Academics or researchers typically do many grant projects before enrolling themselves in an actual PhD.

A large percentage of PhD outcomes don't even get to see its application in corporations unless an intermediate step of converting a PhD into the applied outcome is taken. It is also believed that PhD researchers tend to work on unrealistic issues or problems perceived from a theoretical standpoint and not real business problems. But the common observation is that, organizations struggle to apply the results of PhD studies to their

THE ANATOMY OF A DOCTORATE JOURNEY

corporate settings. They usually do not get the value of sponsoring their managers or leaders for such programs. Organizations require practical knowledge that can be applied to solve a problem or challenge. They need solutions, strategies, systems, and practices. That is how professional doctoral programs evolved.

A professional doctorate addresses the needs from a more practical standpoint. Both my degrees are professional degrees and not academic PhDs. In a professional doctorate, managers are trained through effective coursework if they have never done research before. Typically, managers or people who are in business are not researchers by profession. They possibly have never done any research in their career earlier. So, these professional doctoral degrees allow them to take some time to study certain subjects or courses in detail so that they can understand the foundation of research.

Southern Cross University, Australia, describes the differentiation of a Professional doctorate over a standard PhD as follows: It [professional doctorate] is particularly designed to allow high-achieving business managers, business owners, and senior public servants (who possess a Master's degree) to develop their research skills (via solid training in business research methods) and a project (as a research thesis) that will have practical implications for the industry sector or individual business they belong to. [Source: https://www.scu.edu.au/study-at-scu/courses/doctor-of-business-administration-1447187/]

Now, I wouldn't imagine corporate professionals, managers, CEOs, and leaders daily reading journals or articles or

PLAN YOUR DOCTORATE JOURNEY SMARTLY

information on the latest research. So, there is a good possibility that the problem you are going to solve has to come from your surroundings. So, a professional doctorate might be a way for you to start with. You have already seen the problems surrounding you in your workplace. You already know the kind of problems would give short-term value and which ones would give you long-term value. You also know what kind of problems you're going to solve, and which ones will have a competitive edge.

As a corporate professional, the right-hand side of the spectrum applies to you. That is where you will bring value because you already see worthwhile problems in your surroundings that can give you a long-term competitive edge. You don't have to go anywhere else to find the problem. They are right in front of you.

3.1.7 CONSIDER ALL FACTORS

There are 10 factors under 5 categories (by focus, by tenure, by structure, by assessment, and by mode) that you need to consider while deciding on the structure of the program you would like to pick. Then you should search for a program that matches those preferences. Different universities offer different kinds of programs. Therefore, be aware of what the overall journey will look like. Each of these factors will determine the difficulty level of the challenges you're going to face in your journey.

3.2 ESTIMATE THE TIME

Estimating time investment in the program

How long is this journey?

I thought I was a rock star when I started doing my doctorate. I thought I had been working on my chosen subject for several years and, therefore, far ahead of others. I thought it would be a cakewalk for me and hoped that I would finish in 3 years. But it took me 7 years. Some unexpected challenges will derail your plans.

Here are some data from two different sources. Both are pretty consistent.

Based on the Survey of Earned Doctorates conducted among graduates who received their doctoral degree in 2017, the median time to attain the degree was found to be 5.8 years. While the median time to complete the doctoral program in engineering and science streams tended to be on the shorter side, the median time in arts/humanities was found to be 7.1 years.

Based on a survey conducted by Cornell University, it was found that the average time taken to complete a doctorate is approximately 5.8–6.8 years. Humanities/social sciences take longer than engineering/physical sciences. They also cited a dropout rate of 27%.

The bottom line is that, in the field of humanities/business, because of the subjective nature, it takes about 7 years to complete a doctoral degree. On the other hand, a PhD in engineering or science is relatively faster. The median time is about 6 years.

Let's do a little math.

Course work—1 year

Thesis—3 to 4 years

Assessment/Degree—1 year

Book—1 year

You are going to need about 7 years to make the first value out of your doctoral program. Here is the general breakdown of the efforts.

3.2.1 THESIS WORK

Let's say that you're going to go for a doctoral degree, which comprises coursework and a thesis. It is going to take you about a year for the coursework and about 3–4 years for the thesis. Even if you target 4 years, the chances of running into "scope creep" are high. It will extend your tenure to 5, 6, or even 7 years in total. In fact, finishing the program in a span of 5–6 years is considered an accelerated module.

3.2.2 ASSESSMENT WORK

Even if you write your thesis very quickly, the assessment takes time. The assessment is the heart of the doctoral program. Once you have finished your thesis, it is going to go to your supervisor for review. It will then go to your co-supervisor, who typically comes from a university. It is most likely that both the supervisor and the co-supervisor will tell you to make a lot of amendments to the thesis, even if you consider it to be finalized from your angle. You are going to need to spend a lot of time to really put together some efforts in making the amendments.

Once the necessary amendments are made, they search for a suitable examiner for the thesis, typically from the area in which you have done the research. If your thesis is on a very specialized topic, it is going to be hard to find a suitable examiner. If the university is unable to locate a willing and suitable examiner in your area of research, they are going to proceed with more general specialists who are working in a broader area. In that case, several processes are involved in getting the examiner's consent. Once the examiner gives his/her consent, it takes about 2 months for him/her to review the thesis. As part of this process, examiners provide you with certain feedback. The feedback is extremely critical and comprises several inputs, criticism, critiques, and several questions for you to clarify. Most examiners are well-respected, top-notch experts in their respective fields. So, you can expect a detailed critique of your research.

You are going to need to have a couple of months to prepare the responses to satisfy the examiners. The concerned university will analyze your responses to assess if they are scholarly enough.

PLAN YOUR DOCTORATE JOURNEY SMARTLY

Depending upon the university, there can be several such layers and logistic milestones before you get through. So, you must be aware that this entire process of assessment takes much longer before the university awards the degree. This assessment, which typically spans over a year, is perhaps the most painful phase in the journey to obtaining a doctorate.

3.2.3   PREPARING FOR A BOOK

After you're done with this, you're going to write a book about it, hopefully. Writing a book out of a doctoral thesis is not mandatory. It usually comes automatically; while you spend 7 years researching a topic, you will be driven by your newly found wisdom to create a book out of it.

Book publishing is a different ball game, however. Publishers won't usually accept a thesis as it is most of the time. They are going to ask you to make some changes to turn it into a book format that has value and a message. So, the book typically comes into the planning stage already during the research.

If you do not have a flair for writing a book immediately, then you're going to need to at least publish a substantial number of articles in reputed journals to make sure that you have that scholarly positioning before your thesis goes for assessment.

Because of the above factors, several things need to be completed at the trailing end. It is obviously a difficult phase, and you're going to have to have the patience to go through that.

3.3 ASSESS THE LEVEL OF EFFORTS

Assessing what it takes and the challenges to expect

I wish to share the results of an interesting survey conducted by Nature magazine among 6000 students pursuing PhD. At the beginning of the program, the students were asked how satisfied were they with their decision to pursue the program. Some selected results of the survey are shown in Figure 3-3. About 37% said they were somewhat satisfied, and 38% said they were fully satisfied. The students were then asked mid-way through the program. About 50% of them said that the program was tougher than expected. The other 50% said that they felt the program to be easier and that things improved based on their topic, ecosystem, supervisor, university, and other factors. The point is, it is like flipping the coins. It also means that if you go to people and you ask them about their experience of doing a doctorate, the chances are that you would not have enough conclusive results. It can be a chance game.

Therefore, you need to make "smart choices" about your program in terms of when, where, how, with whom, why, what type, etc. While making those choices, you need to be aware of what might stop your progress. My purpose in this segment is to put you all in a reflective mode so that you guys really prepare yourselves to pay attention to the different possible factors that you may encounter on your way. Some of those factors are going to support you, while some are going to hamper you.

PLAN YOUR DOCTORATE JOURNEY SMARTLY

Reflect on this and capture your notes in Reflection 3.1.

- What are the challenges that you foresee to hamper you during your doctoral journey?
- Are they time, job, family, money, profession, and/or skills?

THE ANATOMY OF A DOCTORATE JOURNEY

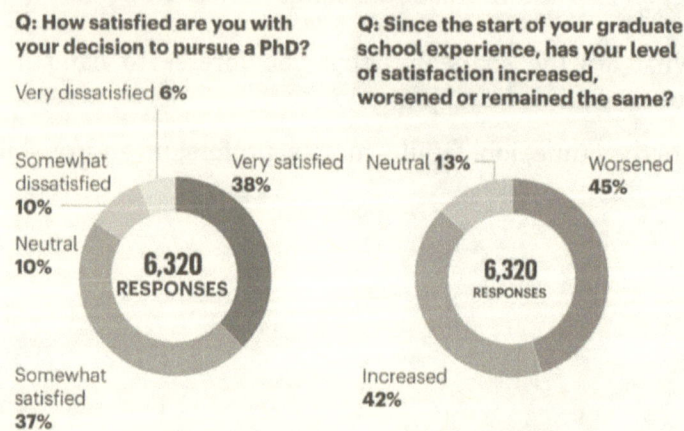

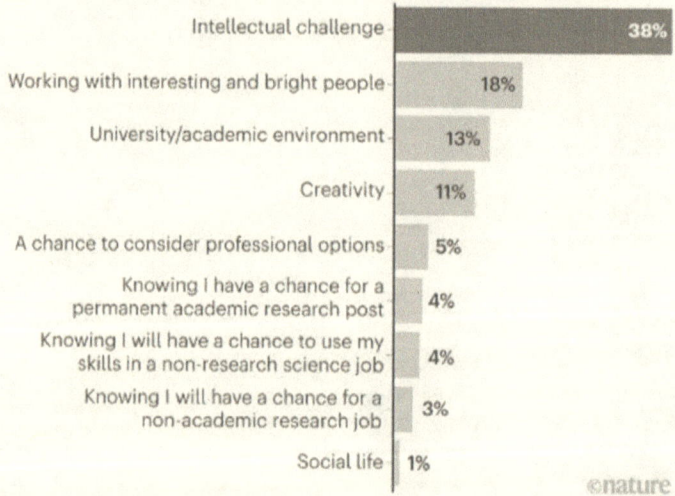

Figure 3-3: Student survey before and during a doctoral program [Source: Nature, Chris Woolston, Nov 2019].

PLAN YOUR DOCTORATE JOURNEY SMARTLY

Reflection 3.1

What are the challenges that you foresee to hamper you during your doctoral journey? Are they time, job, family, money, profession, and/or skills?

THE ANATOMY OF A DOCTORATE JOURNEY

I have listed below some of the challenges based on my experience:

3.3.1 LEARNING NEW SKILLS

You will face the challenge of learning new skills at a faster rate. You're going to need to do research. You're going to need to do an analysis. You're going to need to do a lot of other things. You're going to need several other skills and should be able willing to learn them. So, there will be lots of effort required.

3.3.2 WORK-LIFE BALANCE

Managing the work–life balance is going to be difficult! This is something you're going to need to be aware of right from the beginning, as you have a job, work, or business to do to make money. Therefore, you need to be very sure about how much pressure is going to come on you when you take up this program. You may have to live a new norm, like extended daily hours. The day I started my doctorate, my wife told me that she is pregnant. Now, imagine that! I just started my doctorate, the first day of my doctorate. And by the time I finished my doctorate, it was the sixth birthday of my kid. I spent the entire early childhood of my kid in doing research. It is pretty difficult. Besides that, I'm a full-time corporate manager. I work at least 12 hours a day, and doing the doctorate part-time, in parallel. It has caused more challenges to my work-life balance. Resolving them and trying to strike a balance required a lot of effort.

PLAN YOUR DOCTORATE JOURNEY SMARTLY

3.3.3 READING ARTICLES ENDLESSLY

Reading articles endlessly is going to be an enormous challenge because you may not have had the habit of reading academic journals or academic articles in the past. It is going to be an intensive process.

3.4 FIGURE OUT THE SKILLS

Figure out 6 critical skills required to be successful

Now, a doctorate is a different ballgame from the kind of work you do daily. So, there is a good possibility that you may not have the skills that are required to live with such a tedious program. Let us do some assessment.

Reflect on this for a moment and capture it in Reflection 3.2.

- What are the skills you think you need to complete your doctoral journey?

PLAN YOUR DOCTORATE JOURNEY SMARTLY

Reflection 3.2

In your view, what are the skills you think you need to complete your doctoral journey?

THE ANATOMY OF A DOCTORATE JOURNEY

There are two distinct sets of skills you are going to need to become successful in your doctoral journey.

3.4.1 PROFESSIONAL SKILLS

Based on my experience, there are three professional skills you are going to need in this journey, as shown in Figure 3-4.

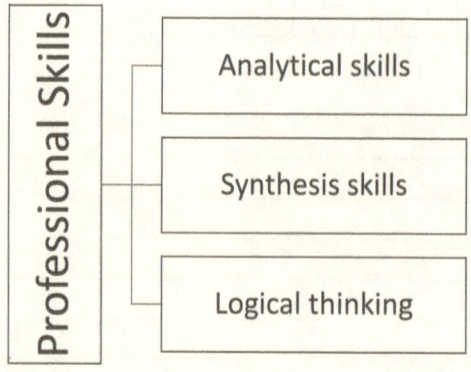

Figure 3-4: The professional skills that you need in your doctoral journey.

a) *Analytical skills*

The most important virtue that is required is that you need to be analytical. It is about breaking a whole idea into pieces, breaking down a problem into its constituent pieces, and seeing how problems, situations, relationships, processes, or abstract observations are composed. Essentially, it is your detailed orientation. This ability is going to be your best friend during the early phases of the journey.

PLAN YOUR DOCTORATE JOURNEY SMARTLY

b) Synthesis skills

The next important virtue that is required is that you should be able to put different pieces of a puzzle into one whole piece, model, or framework. You should be able to see a bigger picture. This ability comes as your best friend to accomplish the outcome you desire.

c) Logical skills

The third important virtue that is required is that you should be logical. Being "logical" means the ability to look at different pieces, or even random things and chaos, and be able to understand or establish relationships among them. You can connect different things together to draw conclusions. Why did a thing happen that way? You should be able to go to the next level way past the analytical skills, able to locate factors that determine the order or effect of some kind. And then, you should be able to draft an argument to explain how that explains something collectively. This ability will come as your best friend when developing models and writing a thesis to academic standards.

Reflect on this and capture your thoughts in Reflection 3.3.

- Which of these skills are you using in your job?
- What is your best bet?

Reflection 3.3

Which of these skills are you using in your job? What is your best bet?

PLAN YOUR DOCTORATE JOURNEY SMARTLY

3.4.2 PERSONAL SKILLS

Now, on the personal side, you're going to need another set of skills. The three important skills you should leverage or build upon as shown in Figure 3-5.

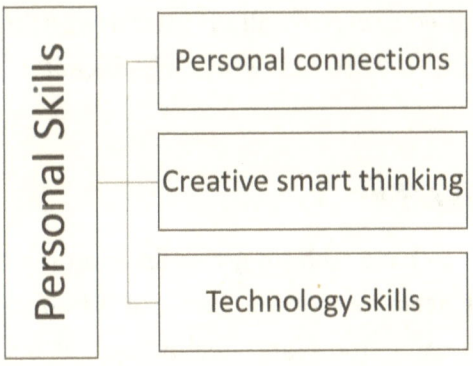

Figure 3-5: The personal skills that you need in your doctoral journey.

a) Personal connections

The most important personal skill that you need is "personal connection." None of the books will tell you that you're going to need this skill. A doctoral program cannot be done in isolation. Personal connection refers to how well you are able to connect with the research participants, the research problem itself, and your supervisors. Are you able to build rapport with all of them within your environment? That is the foremost personal skill that will help you survive this tiresome journey.

THE ANATOMY OF A DOCTORATE JOURNEY

b) *Creative and smart thinking*

At this stage in your life, you don't want to go the hard way. So, you need to be creative in smart thinking. What smart working tools do you need to capture your overwhelming ideas? You have very limited pockets of me-time! How are you going to use your smart thinking to make the best use of that time?

For example, I used to capture all my interviews using mind maps and speech-to-text software, which significantly lessened my manual work.

c) *Technology skills*

Last, you need to have technology skills, even if you are a non-tech guy. You need to see how you can automate or execute certain things using tools and technology. Why do I call it personal skill and not professional? The reason is that you may not be doing a job that requires "technology" skills. For example, if you are required to read hundreds of PDFs/published journal articles, you can use what is called text-to-speech while you're driving. Imagine that you can actually listen to 5 or 10 PDF articles when you're driving.

You need to be aware of these smart technology tools. Another example is, suppose you're going to have a lot of data to interpret. Are you going to analyze them manually, or are you going to use some automated software to interpret them? These are the kind of things you need to adopt.

Reflect on this and capture your observations in Reflection 3.4:

- What personal skills do you have that are very strong?

PLAN YOUR DOCTORATE JOURNEY SMARTLY

Reflection 3.4

What personal skills do you have that are very strong?

3.5 STAY OPEN TO FEEDBACK

Now, as I have been saying throughout this book, you need to make smart choices. But those choices won't come in isolation. You will need to seek feedback from multiple people and multiple sources, such as your peers, classmates, supervisor, boss, or even your spouse.

CHAPTER 4

ASSESSING YOUR BEST BETS AND LEVERAGES

YOUR BEST BETS AND LEVERAGES

In this chapter, learners will be guided through a systematic process to understand and identify what they really need in order to successfully take up a doctoral journey. They will then apply a framework to understand the key strengths or leverages that they can use to make their journey more efficient.

PLAN YOUR DOCTORATE JOURNEY SMARTLY

4.1 KNOW YOUR PERSONALITY

Questioning if you are cut for the program

Am I cut for the same?

The doctoral program is full of hurdles that may not be everyone's cup of tea. So, it is very important that you assess the hardships before embarking on the program.

We talked about professional and personal skills earlier. Most commonly, these are skills many of you would already possess because of your training and the profession that you are associated with. As corporate professionals thinking of attaining a top-notch degree, I bet you already must have been a master of those skills to a great degree—no doubt about that.

However, possessing these top-notch skills alone will not be enough. We have seen people with powerful communication skills. We have seen brilliant people with great connections in the industry. We have seen CEOs of Fortune 500 companies who are creative, intelligent thinkers, and tech-savvy. But not all of them are cut for the PhD journey, even if they wish to. The reality is that several of these highly skilled people quit PhDs halfway.

There is one significant thing you are going to need. That one thing that makes the real difference is the "personality." The personality is the integrator that integrates your professional skills with your personal skills, as shown in Figure 4-1.

The core characteristics of "personality" are:

YOUR BEST BETS AND LEVERAGES

- Your attitude and mindset
- Your navigation skills through odds
- Your approach to the problem and to finding the solution
- Your thought process
- Your ability to deal with/manage stress
- Your ability to persist despite failures

Reflect on this and note down your thoughts in Reflection 4.1:

- Where do you think your personality is cut for this journey?

PLAN YOUR DOCTORATE JOURNEY SMARTLY

Reflection 4.1

Where do you think your personality is cut for this journey?

YOUR BEST BETS AND LEVERAGES

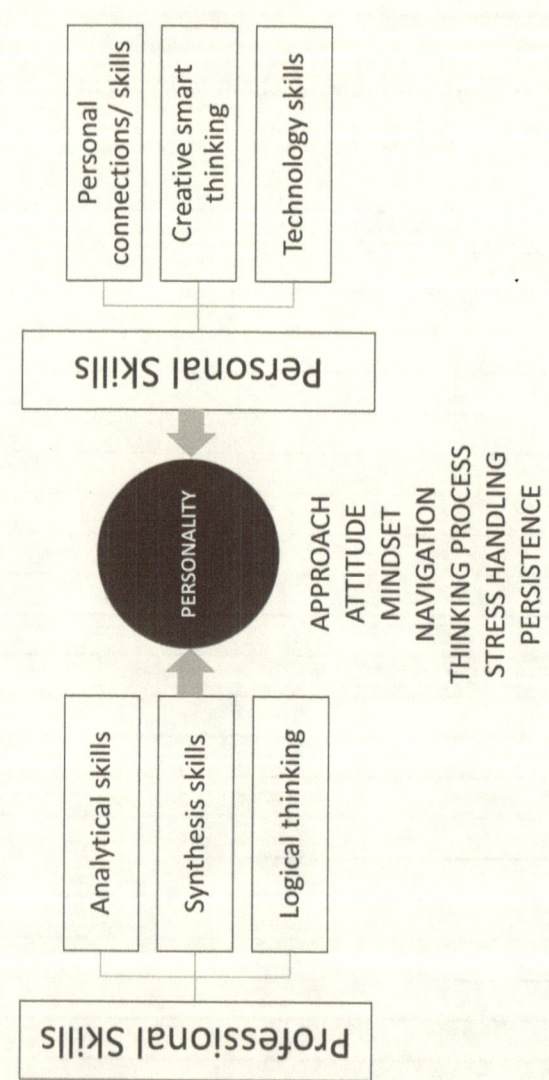

Figure 4-1: Personality as an integrator.

PLAN YOUR DOCTORATE JOURNEY SMARTLY

4.2 LEVERAGE YOUR BEST BETS

Syncing your professional thinking process

The best leverages you have are the years and years of management and leadership indoctrination that you have received while doing your job in organizations. In fact, based on my experience as a practice leader, I feel that you will need nothing more to successfully complete your journey (Figure 4-2).

4.2.1   GOAL-ORIENTED MANAGEMENT

The first and foremost of your best bet is what you do when you get a big project or an initiative. You focus on the goals. When you get into a problem, you keep thinking, what's my goal? Every time you run into a problem, you think of a solution or tool that can lead you to achieve that goal. In a research study, if you have that goal orientation, you could do it in a really efficient manner.

4.2.2   PRAGMATIC APPROACHES

The second one is what we use almost every single day in our job. Pragmatism's simple definition is "what works." As a manager, when you run into an issue or when you need to find a solution, you ask a simple question, "what works here?" You ask, "given the situations, resources, time, and goals, how best can I complete this?" You don't read tens of leadership or management books to frame your approach. Essentially, you think practically, pragmatically, and not in the textbook way.

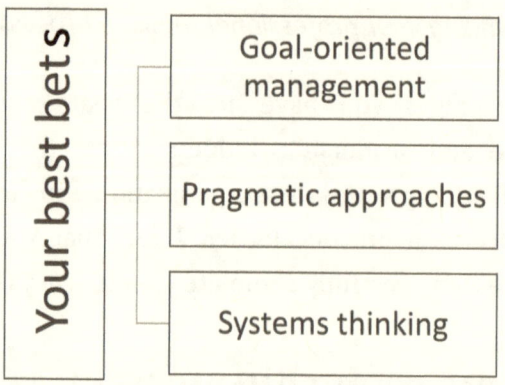

Figure 4-2: Your best bets.

4.2.3 SYSTEMS THINKING

The third one is what we all commonly use. Systems thinking is something like this: this is my input A, which is feeding a system of things or processes. I need to control condition C to get the desired output B. If my output B is not up to the desired standards, I will vary condition C or change input A. This "closed-loop" method of how things process together to create the desired output is one of the critical mechanisms for completing a PhD.

Let's reflect on this. Capture your thinking in Reflection 4.2.

- What is your best bet in your current job/profession or otherwise?

PLAN YOUR DOCTORATE JOURNEY SMARTLY

Reflection 4.2

What is your best bet in your current job/profession or otherwise?

4.3 FIND THE KEY LEVERAGES

Scouting 3 types of leverages from various dimensions of your personality

You will likely have many of the personal, professional, and technological leverages that you are using in your career or profession. However, you need to identify all those leverages in order to use them strategically and smartly to complete your doctoral journey effortlessly.

4.3.1 TECHNOLOGICAL LEVERAGES

Some of the technological leverages that one might possess are shown in Figure 4-3.

Some of you may have good advanced Excel skills. Some of you may already have the ability to do data analytics. Some of you are already doing data visualization when you present your research to your executive management. In a doctoral study, you will usually get a massive amount of data if you're doing good quantitative research. If you are already good at data visualization, then you may be able to apply that tool to complete your research.

Many of you may be already aware of the various survey software available. You can apply some or all of them to your research project to make sense of participant responses and come up with themes.

PLAN YOUR DOCTORATE JOURNEY SMARTLY

Similarly, some of you may already know about high-end machine learning (ML) or Artificial Intelligence (AI). Several research projects utilize AI to conduct data analysis.

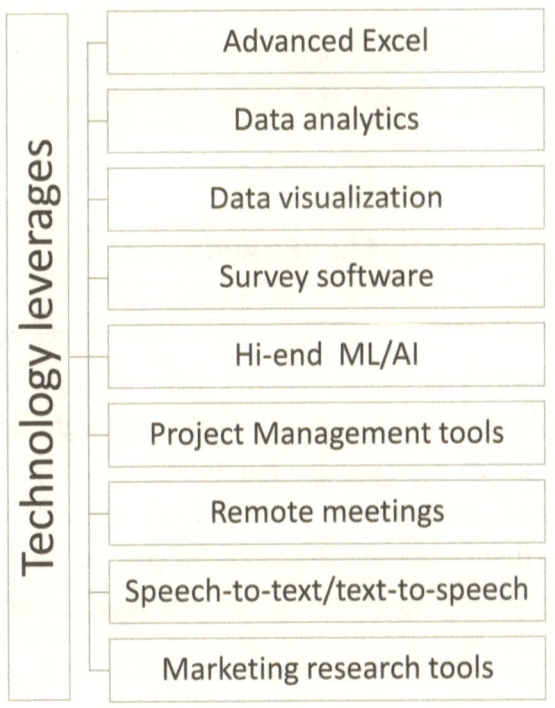

Figure 4-3: Technology leverages.

Some of you may have good experience using project management tools, software, or methods. You can use some of them to manage your doctoral journey.

Many of you may already be experts at running remote meetings as part of your job profile. So, you can use these applications to

YOUR BEST BETS AND LEVERAGES

recruit your participants and run all the research interviews remotely, just like how you conduct your meetings.

Similarly, some of you may have used speech-to-text or text-to-speech tools to shorten your efforts.

If you have exposure to any of these tools or technologies in your current job, you can apply them appropriately in your doctoral journey.

4.3.2   ECOSYSTEM LEVERAGES

Similar to technological leverages, several leverages come from your ecosystem, too. By ecosystem, I mean what surrounds you at your workplace. On several occasions, you might not have to learn completely new things, but look around you in your ecosystem and figure out your leverages. Once you identify them, you can use them to resolve the problems you will be working on and even find the people who will support your research.

Some of those ecosystem leverages are shown in Figure 4-4. If you are working in a corporate or business setting, you are likely to be surrounded by several problems. You're going to pick one of those compelling problems for your doctoral research. When you do so, you will have credibility.

In the professional world, you have certain designations and job titles. When you use those titles, people are going to listen to you, and they're going to be willing to participate in your research.

PLAN YOUR DOCTORATE JOURNEY SMARTLY

Your connections may be used as leverages, too. In some cases, you may have quality people in your connections who would be the ideal candidates to support you or participate in your research. Why don't you have them as your participants?

If you are active on social media, then you could publicize your research and use social media as a way to gather information.

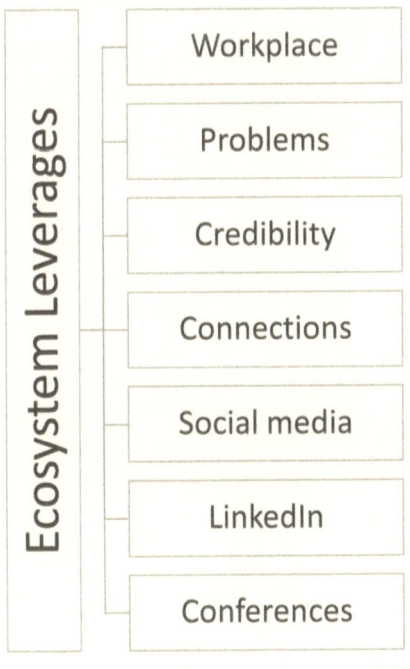

Figure 4-4: Ecosystem leverages.

YOUR BEST BETS AND LEVERAGES

4.3.3 PERSONAL LEVERAGES

There are personal leverages as well that spring up because of your unique approaches or opportunities. Some of those are shown in Figure 4-5.

You also have personal leverages such as your background, techniques, and style, among other things.

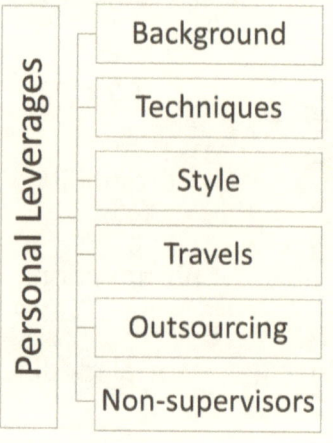

Figure 4-5: Personal leverages.

For instance, I tend to talk a lot qualitatively. When I went for my doctorate, I leveraged this tendency to talk to people. So, I took up qualitative research, which involved a lot of in-depth conversations with the participants. I leveraged my style for my doctoral research.

I used to travel a lot. That helped me a lot because I could meet with some of the leaders/eminent people in the fields of my

PLAN YOUR DOCTORATE JOURNEY SMARTLY

study. I attended several international conferences and got to meet specialists there as well. Thus, I leveraged my travel opportunities to really connect with people.

Few people may guide you about using "outsourcing" to your advantage. For instance, one of the challenges that I faced was the unique citation style or reference style that I was asked to follow in my thesis. It would have been extremely taxing if I had to incorporate the reference style manually. So, I hired a freelancer from Upwork, a freelancing platform. I paid about $50 to $100 to the freelancer to develop an automated citation and referencing software that generated output as needed by the university. I did the whole citation and referencing task using the software, which otherwise would have taken several months. If you know how to work with freelancers, there are different parts of your doctoral journey that you can outsource and get done.

As I explained in the previous chapters, you are going to need several synthesis skills to integrate different pieces together to complete your doctoral journey.

No doubt, you are going to depend upon your thesis supervisors. But, that alone may not be enough. For example, in my case, I had six non-supervising guides who were constantly guiding me, reviewing my data, reviewing my findings, and giving feedback on what made sense and what did not. So, you can draw upon qualified people from your network.

Reflect on this and capture your responses in Reflection 4.3:

- What "levers" can you pull? What leverages are available to you to complete this journey smartly, creatively, and efficiently with the lesser hassle, hard work, or effort?

YOUR BEST BETS AND LEVERAGES

Reflection 4.3

What "levers" can you pull? What leverages are available to you to complete this journey smartly, creatively, and efficiently with the lesser hassle, hard work, or effort?

4.4 PERSONALITY & ECOSYSTEM

Your leverages come from different dimensions of your personality and the things your ecosystem offers you. When you make the best use of these two assets, you can probably complete your doctoral journey with much ease.

CHAPTER 5

HOW TO START THE JOURNEY WITH THE END IN MIND

THE JOURNEY WITH THE END IN MIND

This is the most important and a high-value chapter of this book. Here, you will learn how to choose the area of research smartly and how to narrow down your topic of research that brings value to your personal and professional lives. You will learn to use systems tools to make more informed decisions that can ensure that your doctoral program is not only of high value but also is being pursued with least effort.

PLAN YOUR DOCTORATE JOURNEY SMARTLY

5.1 CHOOSE THE RIGHT MODE

Selecting the best mode or type of program that works for you

My philosophy is that "in order to start the journey, you have to put your best foot forward." That means you should understand how you can complete your journey effortlessly and how you will be able to achieve what you are hoping for out of this program.

The first and foremost thing that is important is selecting the correct model and type of doctoral program you're going to go to. Here, you have a lot of parameters to consider.

5.1.1 TYPE

In the previous chapters, we discussed the different journey types. So, which one do you want to do? Do you want to do a PhD, professional doctorate, or a DBA?

5.1.2 STRUCTURE

Are you going to go for a coursework-based doctorate, thesis-based doctorate, or both?

THE JOURNEY WITH THE END IN MIND

5.1.3 TENURE

Here, your choice as a working professional is obviously going to be for a part-time degree.

5.1.4 UNIVERSITY

The university is a very important place. Are you going to go for an international or a local one?

5.1.5 STANDING

Just to be aware of university standing. Because the doctorate is the highest degree and is most likely to be the last degree that you pursue, it is bound to make a long-lasting impression. That name is always going to stay with you! So, choose a reputed university. Should you go to a high-end, Ivy League-type university? Or you could choose a mid-tier university? In my opinion, top-tier is not a must. Choose a university that has a good standing. You don't necessarily need to go to top-tier universities because you have already lived your corporate career. Now, all you're looking for is a competitive edge that comes with the wisdom you're going to draw out of this program. Not *per se* the tile of the degree or the university from which you did it.

PLAN YOUR DOCTORATE JOURNEY SMARTLY

5.1.6 MODE

You can go for this program at the actual university campus or choose an off-campus setup or opt for distance learning, depending on the kind of bandwidth that you have.

5.1.7 THESIS SUPERVISOR

Most universities will provide you with a list of folks who are in their roles as supervisors. You will be able to review their profiles and expertise ahead of time. You will be free to choose the one that aligns with your area of expertise. You would have to talk to several of them to figure out whose personality is in sync with yours. Choosing a guide is a painful little segment of the journey. But, it is extremely important. Choosing the correct guide is going to go a long way.

Whether you're going to choose an academician or industry supervisor—sometimes, you may not have much choice about it. You will have to go by the general guidelines of the university. However, if your topic is more corporate-oriented, you must pick a research guide/supervisor who has good corporate experience. In such scenarios, if you choose an academic supervisor, their standards and viewpoints may be different, hence not advantageous. In some other scenarios, you may not be prepared to go through all the harsh criteria or standards those supervisors have gone through. If you are not a trained researcher, you're going to have many challenges. So, be careful. Look for a program that allows you to choose a corporate supervisor or a combination of both. The academic guide's focus will be more on making sure that the research results you produce are academic and scholarly in nature, whereas the corporate guide is going to ensure that the knowledge you are producing is useful. In my case, the university gave me a corporate supervisor and an academic supervisor. It was a great combination. It was very important to me as I wanted a supervisor who has lived his corporate life so that he could understand the kind of problem I was trying to solve. My corporate supervisor did not push me to write articles. Rather, he was more interested in creating useful knowledge for the corporate world. Once I had that alignment, the overall program progressed smoothly. Otherwise, it could have been a lot more complicated. You must align with the supervisor beforehand because getting through those conflicts is very difficult at the later stages. The bottom line is that you need to be able to 'manage the supervisor.'

Also, the credibility of the guide is very important. When your thesis goes on for an assessment, it makes a quick difference if you have done a thesis under a well-known, credible person in that wisdom circle. If yes, you already got an edge.

5.1.8 LIBRARY RESOURCES

You're also going to need to look at the library facilities offered by the university you have in mind. You're going to need to read a lot. You should know whether you got an online library available to you by the university. This is a very important piece, which few people think about at the outset. Many of the universities have only physical libraries. Of course, many of them have gone digital. All in all, you're going to need an online one.

5.1.9 ASSESSMENT

Are you good at presentations? Can you defend your ideas in front of top-notch assessors? Or, are you great at writing? So, select a university or program that aligns well with your existing skill set. When you are on your doctoral journey, you may not have enough time to learn new skills. Therefore, you've got to leverage what you already have to the best possible level.

5.2 SELECT A CREDIBLE AREA OF RESEARCH

Through my two doctorates, I came up with a sort of framework regarding how to really go through selecting the most appropriate area of research for a doctoral program.

If you're already a corporate professional with 10 or 20 years of experience, you already have tons of ideas. You have worked in several different jobs. You may have built several specializations. And you may have seen a variety of problems throughout your career. As you look back, everything may seem very appealing and worth researching.

Here is one simple way of looking at things in a little more rational way. If you are a systems-thinking person or think pragmatically or a goal-oriented manager, you need a systematic, criteria-driven approach.

It is a simple matrix! A sample of this is shown in Figure 5-1. You list down all the functional areas you have worked on in the past or all the functional areas that appeal to you today.

PLAN YOUR DOCTORATE JOURNEY SMARTLY

	SIGNIFICANT CAREER STREAMS	TOP-NOTCH SKILLS OR SPECIALIZATION	AUTHORITY, EXPERTISE, RECOGNITIONS, CREDENTIALS	WORK, EXPERIMENT, MODELS CREATED DURING THE COURSE OF EMPLOYMENT OR BUSINESS	AUTHORSHIPS OR PUBLICATIONS	PASSIONS, MOTIVATIONS AND INTERESTS	FUTURE PROFESSIONAL OR PERSONAL PROSPECTS
Functional Area 1	x	x		x		x	x
Functional Area 2	x	x	x	x	x		
Functional Area 3	x		x				
Functional Area 4							
Functional Area 5					x		
Functional Area 6	x	x	x	x			
Functional Area 7	x	x	x				
Functional Area 8			x				
Functional Area 9	x	x	x	x		x	
Functional Area 10	x				x		
Functional Area 11	x	x	x			x	x

Figure 5-1: Matrix for selecting a credible area of research

THE JOURNEY WITH THE END IN MIND

5.2.1 SIGNIFICANT CAREER STREAMS

The first thing for you to look at is whether you have actually spent a significant amount of your career in the desired functional area. If yes, put a tick across that cell.

5.2.2 TOP-NOTCH SKILLS OR SPECIALIZATION

The next step is to look at whether you have the top-notch skills or specialization in that functional area or not. If yes, put a tick across.

5.2.3 AUTHORITY, EXPERTISE, OR CREDENTIALS

Then look at whether you already hold some authority, expertise, recognition, or credentials in that functional area. This is going to build your credibility. Imagine with that particular topic in hand. You're going to go to some big-shot leaders or corporate professionals and appeal to them to participate in your research. However, if you don't hold authority in that functional area yet, you need to think of other appealing reasons to select that area.

5.2.4 INTELLECTUAL PROPERTY CREATED

Then look at the fact whether you already have some sort of work done in that area. For example, perhaps, you have created some models, done some experiments through your profession, consulting, practice, talks, or speaking engagements. If you have

PLAN YOUR DOCTORATE JOURNEY SMARTLY

created a framework already, it may be a good candidate for you to take it forward into the doctoral research. You may have created your own IP or wisdom in that area. Put a tick across those criteria.

5.2.5 AUTHORSHIPS OR PUBLICATIONS

Next, look at whether you have already published an article or written a book on a given functional area.

5.2.6 PASSIONS OR MOTIVATIONS

Next comes passion/motivation. You also need to be very sure about your passion. If you're very passionate about a topic and very motivated about it, a doctoral degree program is a place to live that passion. Remember, you will be in the program for 7 years. It is more meaningful to spend that much time on an idea you are truly passionate about. The program will force you to read every single article and every single book out there on that idea. Just imagine the level of transformation or wisdom you will acquire through 7 years of focused reading on one particular idea. That idea is going to distill into wisdom. The program is going to force you to come up with something innovative out of it. This is the part that will allow your passion to become a business, and you can share that innovation with a larger public in the form of a framework, model, or theory. It then eventually becomes your business.

THE JOURNEY WITH THE END IN MIND

5.2.7   FUTURE PROSPECTS

What are the personal or professional prospects that you can derive from a particular topic? This is where you need to think about the fact whether your idea or outcome will be relevant even after 7 to 14 years? Can you make value out of the idea at that time? Can you get enough financial returns from the program that probably cost you at least $100,000?

And, once you have done some exercise for all the potential functional areas, you can score it or put a scale of 1 to 10. But the idea is to see if you got the most number of ticks against one or more functional areas. Then, you should prioritize and compare those potential areas to select the one that works the best for your goals.

You can use the blank matrix in Figure 5-2 to evaluate your potential research areas. Once you narrow down 1-3 broader areas, you can use Reflection 5.1 to score the best scoring broader area.

PLAN YOUR DOCTORATE JOURNEY SMARTLY

	SIGNIFICANT CAREER STREAMS	TOP-NOTCH SKILLS OR SPECIALIZATION	AUTHORITY, EXPERTISE, RECOGNITIONS, CREDENTIALS	WORK, EXPERIMENT, MODELS CREATED DURING THE COURSE OF EMPLOYMENT OR BUSINESS	AUTHORSHIPS OR PUBLICATIONS	PASSIONS, MOTIVATIONS AND INTERESTS	FUTURE PROFESSIONAL OR PERSONAL PROSPECTS
Functional Area 1							
Functional Area 2							
Functional Area 3							
Functional Area 4							
Functional Area 5							
Functional Area 6							
Functional Area 7							
Functional Area 8							
Functional Area 9							
Functional Area 10							

Figure 5-2: Sample matrix to evaluate your research areas

THE JOURNEY WITH THE END IN MIND

Reflection 5.1

Derving a list of broader areas of research			
Criterion	Broader area #1	Broader area #2	Broader area #3
(1) Significant career streams			
(2) Top-notch skills or specialization			
(3) Authority, expertise, recognitions, credentials			
(4) Work, experiments, and models created			
(5) Authorship of publications			
(6) Passions, motivations, and interests			
(7) Future personal or professional prospects			
Score			

PLAN YOUR DOCTORATE JOURNEY SMARTLY

5.3 SELECTING A REWARDING TOPIC

Systematically selecting the most rewarding topic for your research

Once you have selected the main area of research, how do you select a high-value topic? For that, I recommend using more detailed criteria. An example shown here is an actual table that I used for selecting the topic of my research.

After I narrowed down my functional area, I discovered several potential topics within that functional area to pursue my research. Obviously, it was not an easy decision because everything looked so appealing to me at that time. That's where you need to apply systems thinking.

At this point, I was looking into the potential challenges I may have running with each topic. Remember, once I chose, I would have to run with it for over 5–7 years. The point is obviously not to avoid but to be aware of what may be in the store down the line once the research council approves your topic. Here are some key considerations against which you may want to assess each of the potential topics.

Topic authority: Why you?

- Technical experience in the relevant domain
- Expertise and skill in the topic

Research authority: Why this way?

THE JOURNEY WITH THE END IN MIND

- Experience in the chosen methodology
- Relevant experience in research

Motivations and drivers: Why do it?

- Targeted or desired outcomes
- Why—personal motivation

Ecosystem: Why only this?

- Leverages or advantages
- Networking/connections
- Style of working

Efforts: Why not this?

- Challenges or pitfalls
- Limitations or weaknesses
- Time and bandwidth

I listed all the topics in the table's header shown in Figure 5-3, which is a snapshot of the assessment I made for my research study using the above framework. As you read through the columns, you will understand how the last topic gave me several advantages and put me on the path to success.

PLAN YOUR DOCTORATE JOURNEY SMARTLY

5.3.1 TOPIC AUTHORITY: WHY YOU?

The first is about assessing your topic authority, answering the question: Why you? Are you the topic authority? Under each of the topics, I started listing down two things: one is your technical topic or domain experience, and the other is your topic expertise and skills. So, when I lined up these two things across the rows, I got a sense of whether I could justify powerfully that I am the most qualified to do the research on that particular topic.

5.3.2 RESEARCH AUTHORITY: WHY THIS WAY?

The second is about assessing the research authority, which answers the question: Why this way? This is where you need to look at if you have some methodological experience. Let's say that you do have broad experience in research. Are you going to do survey-based quantitative research? Or, are you going to do qualitative research? Do you even have a background in using such methods? Are you good at statistics and probability? If you're going to use qualitative methods, are you good at connecting with people? Have you done it before? Have you talked to 20 people before and come up with some sort of insights out of it? The point here is that research experience matters.

5.3.3 MOTIVATIONS AND DRIVERS: WHY DO IT?

The third one is about motivation and drives, answering the question: Why do it?

I arrived at these questions:

THE JOURNEY WITH THE END IN MIND

Why should I really pursue those motivations?

Is there a strong burning desire inside me to explore it?

What is really pushing me to conduct deeper research in this area?

What is the outcome I'm desiring?

What is my personal motivation?

You need to write them down in a few words to get more clarity.

5.3.4   ECOSYSTEM: WHY ONLY THIS?

The fourth one is about the ecosystem, which answers the question: Why only this? Only a few people actually think about the ecosystem when beginning a doctoral program. Most of us think that we are alone in this journey and that it is my degree and my research, so I need to think only about what I can do. But, in reality, you're going to need to think about the things around you, people around you, what leverages or advantages or x-factors you have. Maybe your title or position in a company or industry already gives you the leverage to do the doctorate far easier. Or, perhaps you've got a good network of people or connections from which you can draw your mentors and supervisor. Maybe your work style is just appropriate for the given topic of research. For instance, I leveraged my work style of interacting with people and being in constant conversations. I used to travel frequently, which was the quietest time away from e-mails. I could make the most of 20 hours of flight time between Singapore and the US and could read 100 different articles during

PLAN YOUR DOCTORATE JOURNEY SMARTLY

the flight. You need to look at your job parameters and the things around the job to figure out how they can support you. All these things are the components of the ecosystem that is available to you.

If you've got four or five topics, you need to be able to answer the question: Why this topic and not anything else? Your ecosystem is going to tell you why you should pick a specific topic.

5.3.5 EFFORTS: WHY NOT THIS?

The fifth one is about the efforts that answer the question: Why not this? This is the place to look out for all the negative things that can potentially challenge or stop you. What challenges are you going to face? What pitfalls are you going to face? What limitations or weaknesses do you anticipate? What type of bandwidth issues may you encounter? For instance, my limitation was that I was not really a mathematical guy. So, I refrained from picking a topic that was a little mathematical in nature. You need to look at several such challenges or reasons as to why you should not pick a particular topic or move in that direction. You need to look at your job. If your job is very hectic, travel-oriented, etc., will you able to spend enough time on your research journey on the desired/selected topic?

You can use the blank template from Figure 5-4 or Reflection 5.3 to evaluate and select a rewarding research topic that you could pursue with all the steam.

Reflect on this and capture your evaluation in Reflection 5.2:

THE JOURNEY WITH THE END IN MIND

- To select a high-value, effortless topic of research, you need to think about five aspects—Why you? Why this way? Why do it? Why only this? And, why not this?

PLAN YOUR DOCTORATE JOURNEY SMARTLY

Reflection 5.2

What are your responses to these five aspects—Why you? Why this way? Why do it? Why only this? And, why not this?

THE JOURNEY WITH THE END IN MIND

Factor	Category	Topic 1	Topic 2	Topic 3	Topic 4
TOPIC AUTHORITY: WHY YOU?	TECHNICAL/ TOPIC/ DOMAIN EXPERIENCE	Domain experience in learning and training for over 15 years	Close to 20 years of domain experience.	Direct troubleshooting and problem-solving experience is lacking	Domain experience in learning and training for over 15 years
	TOPIC EXPERTISE/ SKILLS	Worked on a related project in the last 5 years and handling several aspects of the project, fresh experience	Topic skills are very old on systems engineering and handling product development	Topic experience from a learning design standpoint	Last 5 years involved in time to proficiency and certification, fresh experience
RESEARCH AUTHORITY: WHY THIS WAY?	METHODOLOGICAL EXPERIENCE	Quantitative research may be challenging given weak skills in stats	Never done qualitative research before	Never done qualitative research before	Never done qualitative research before
	GENERAL RESEARCH EXPERIENCE	Served as scientist for 10 years	Served as scientist for 10 years	Served as scientist for 10 years	Served as scientist for 10 years
MOTIVATIONS AND DRIVERS: WHY DO IT?	TARGETED OR DESIRED OUTCOMES	A list of factors or theory	A methodology or framework	A commercially viable model or framework for consulting practice	A commercially viable model or framework for consulting practice
	WHY – PERSONAL MOTIVATION	Relevant to current employment	Demanding area, highly interested in cross-functional domains	Good demand in high-tech industries including my own organization, become an authority	Huge demand, budding area, personal interests in accelerated strategies
ECO-SYSTEM: WHY ONLY THIS?	LEVERAGES OR ADVANTAGES OR X-FACTORS	Within scope to current employment, lesser dependencies outside	None	Within scope to current employment, lesser dependencies outside	My current position may be leveraged to build connections with potential organizations
	NETWORKING/ CONNECTIONS	Generally relevant to several connections, participants can be sourced internally	Very limited people in my network or interactions with expertise	Easy access to participants internally	Credibility to get desired participants
	WORKSTYLE	I am more of a qualitative guy	Involves lots of reading work matching my style	Day to day work has a direct connection with the topic	Involves lots of reading work matching my style
EFFORTS: WHY NOT THIS?	CHALLENGES/ PITFALLS	The knowledge created may be subjected to confidentiality internally,	I don't know how many people with such background, several unknowns, three disciplines involved. Hard to get a supervisor in this area	The knowledge created may be subjected to confidentiality internally, may involve management approvals, Hard to get a supervisor in this area	Budding area, not many experts to reach out but may be interested in collaborating
	LIMITATIONS/ WEAKNESSES	Weak in stats	Applicable to limited use cases like large tech corporation,	The usefulness of research may be limited	Theoretically appealing, practically scope is unknown
	TIME/ BANDWIDTH	May be quite fast, data almost readily available	Cross-functional area between 3 disciplines, may turn out to be a massive effort	Could be quite fast	May take a long time, but I already have the foundation

Figure 5-3: Sample matrix to select a rewarding research topic

PLAN YOUR DOCTORATE JOURNEY SMARTLY

Factor	Category	Topic 1	Topic 2	Topic 3	Topic 4
TOPIC AUTHORITY: WHY YOU?	TECHNICAL/ TOPIC/ DOMAIN EXPERIENCE				
	TOPIC EXPERTISE/ SKILLS				
RESEARCH AUTHORITY: WHY THIS WAY?	METHODOLOGICAL EXPERIENCE				
	GENERAL RESEARCH EXPERIENCE				
MOTIVATIONS AND DRIVERS: WHY DO IT?	TARGETED OR DESIRED OUTCOMES				
	WHY – PERSONAL MOTIVATION				
ECO-SYSTEM: WHY ONLY THIS?	LEVERAGES OR ADVANTAGES OR X-FACTORS				
	NETWORKING/ CONNECTIONS				
	WORKSTYLE				
EFFORTS: WHY NOT THIS?	CHALLENGES/ PITFALLS				
	LIMITATIONS/ WEAKNESSES				
	TIME/ BANDWIDTH				

Figure 5-4: Sample matrix for readers to select a rewarding research topic

THE JOURNEY WITH THE END IN MIND

Reflection 5.3

	Identfying the most suitable topic			
Crtierion	Sub-criterion	Topic #1	Topic #2	Topic #3
(1) Topic authority: Why you?	Technical/topic/domain experience			
	Topic expertise/skills			
(2) Research authority: Why this way?	Methodological experience			
	General research experience			
(3) Motivations and drivers: Why do it?	Targeted or desired outcomes			
	Why—personal motivation			
(4) Ecosystem: Why only this?	Leverages/advantages/x-factors			
	Networks/connections			
	Workstyle			
(5) Efforts: Why not this?	Challenges/pitfalls			
	Limitations/weaknesses			
	Time/bandwidth			

PLAN YOUR DOCTORATE JOURNEY SMARTLY

5.4 MAKE SMART CHOICES

How many of you love traveling or going on a journey?

Have you realized that the quality, fun, enjoyment, and memory of any journey will depend on how well you plan and the smart choices you make?

Similarly, a successful journey for a doctorate is less about going to a certain destination and more about the smart choices you make on the way. One wrong choice can take you tangential and put you to the edge of quitting and frustration, and one smart choice can make the journey so beautiful that you would love to teach others how to make that great choice.

CHAPTER 6

WHAT IS NEXT?

WHAT IS NEXT

Where to go next?

You may have already enrolled in a doctoral program, or you may be contemplating. Irrespective of the stand you take, you will need a lot of guidance during the journey.

PLAN YOUR DOCTORATE JOURNEY SMARTLY

6.1 RESEARCH FRAMEWORK

You will need a framework, which is basically a process, a tested process that can guide you without bogging you down into confusing, unclear methods and abstract writings. An example of a framework is shown in Figure 6-1, which is a step-by-step approach, techniques, guiding questions, and criteria for how you are going to decide about your choices in the research.

As managers or corporate folks, we want absolute clarity. We can't stand confusion. We can't stand when things are fuzzy. And, we can't take up when frameworks or approaches are not clear enough. That's why it is very important to choose a framework that represents the thinking process typically used in organizations. Choosing a framework is out of the scope of this lesson. However, I encourage the learners to take this wisdom one notch up. Look for my upcoming book titled "Speed up your qualitative business research—Start to end research process unpacked step by step." This book is a complete blueprint of how I successfully finished my doctoral study and research dissertation. This 550-p book has been written to handhold practitioners and professionals throughout a business research study.

WHAT IS NEXT

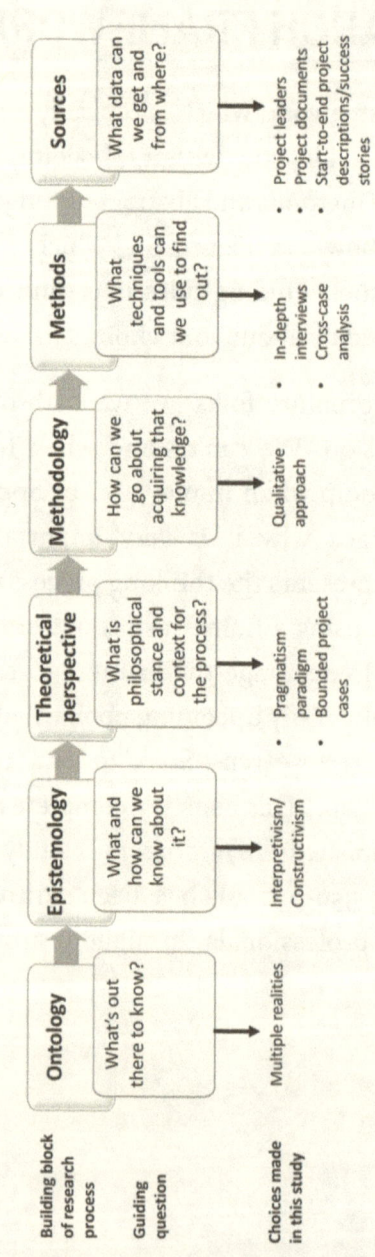

Figure 6-1: An example of research framework helping a doctorate research design

6.2 ONLINE COURSE

If you would like to go over the content of this book as a training course, you can enroll in my 3-hour online course, which is a collection of videos and written resources, including downloadable templates and guides. Check out this link to enroll in the course. https://get-there-faster.com/courses/how-to-decide-and-plan-your-doctorate-degree-path-online/.

FROM THE SAME AUTHOR

DESIGNING TRAINING TO SHORTEN TIME TO PROFICIENCY: Online, Classroom and On-the-Job Learning Strategies from Research

ISBN: 978-981-14-0633-1 (e-book)
ISBN: 978-981-14-0632-4 (paperback)
ISBN: 978-981-14-0645-4 (hardcover)

Available with major retailers, distributors and market places

ACCELERATE YOUR LEADERSHIP DEVELOPMENT IN TRAINING DOMAIN: Proven Success Strategies for New Training & Learning Managers

ISBN: 978-981-11-8991-3 (e-book)
ISBN: 978-981-14-0066-7 (paperback)

Available with major retailers, distributors and market places

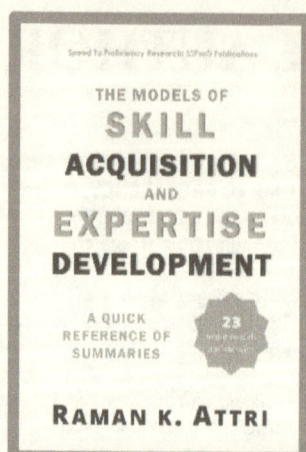

THE MODELS OF SKILL ACQUISITION AND EXPERTISE DEVELOPMENT: A Quick Reference of Summaries

SBN: 978-981-11-8988-3 (e-book)
ISBN: 978-981-14-1122-9 (paperback)
ISBN: 978-981-14-1130-4 (hardcover)

Available with major retailers, distributors and market places

TRAINING EFFECTIVENESS MEASUREMENT FOR LARGE SCALE PROGRAMS: DEMYSTIFIED! A 4-Tier Practical Model for Technical Training Managers

ISBN: 978-981-11-8990-6 (e-book)
ISBN: 978-981-11-417672 (paperback)

Available with major retailers, distributors and market places

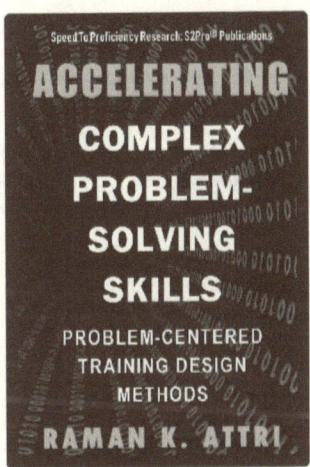

ACCELERATING COMPLEX PROBLEM-SOLVING SKILLS: Problem-Centered Training Design Methods

ISBN: 978-981-11-8991-2 (e-book)
ISBN: 978-981-14-1766-5 (paperback)

Available with major retailers, distributors and market places

SPEED TO PROFICIENCY IN ORGANIZATIONS: Model, Practices and Strategies to Shorten Time To Proficiency

ISBN 978-981-14-0753-6 (e-book)

Available with major retailers, distributors and market places

ACCELERATED PROFICIENCY FOR ACCELERATED TIMES: A Review of Key Concepts and Methods to Speed Up Performance

ISBN: 978-981-14-6276-4 (e-book)
ISBN: 978-981-14-6275-7 (paperback)
ISBN: 978-981-14-6274-0 (hardcover)

Available with major retailers, distributors and market places

SPEED MATTERS: Why best in class business leaders priotize workforce time to proficiency metrics

ISBN: 978-981-18-0536-3 (e-book)
ISBN: 978-981-18-0535-6 (paperback)
ISBN: 978-981-18-0534-9 (hardcover)

Available with major retailers, distributors and market places

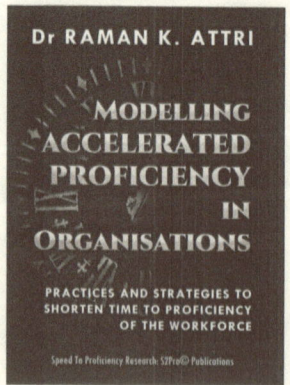

MODELLING ACCELERATED PROFICIENCY IN ORGANISATIONS: Practices and Strategies to shorten time to proficiency of the workforce

ISBN: 978-981-18-4290-0 (e-book)
ISBN: 978-981-18-4288-7 (paperback)
ISBN: 978-981-18-4289-4 (hardcover)

Available with major retailers, distributors and market places

www.ingramcontent.com/pod-product-compliance
Lightning Source LLC
LaVergne TN
LVHW091549070526
838199LV00029B/611/J